Jennifer and Mary Charlotte
Wilcox.

THEIR ROYAL HIGHNESSES

Prince Charles
& Princess Anne

THEIR ROYAL HIGHNESSES

Prince Charles
& Princess Anne

An Authoritative Account by

LADY PEACOCK

HUTCHINSON

Hutchinson & Co. (Publishers) Ltd.

| London | Melbourne | Sydney | Auckland |
| Bombay | Cape Town | New York | Toronto |

First published 1955

Book designed by
KEN WILLIAMSON

Printed in Great Britain by
WILLIAM BRENDON AND SON LTD
THE MAYFLOWER PRESS
(late of Plymouth)
WATFORD

A Marcus Adams portrait : Christmas 1954

THE words 'Princes in the Tower' bring to life a picture of two forlorn and very frightened little boys imprisoned in the Tower of London. These two young brothers who were next in succession to the Throne of England were shut up in the Tower by their uncle, Richard, Duke of Gloucester. Eventually they were murdered by order of their uncle, so that he could ascend the throne and become Richard III of England. These two small princes were by no means the only children in direct line to the throne who lost their lives in mysterious and tragic circumstances. Prince Arthur, heir to Richard I, was thrown into prison by his uncle, John, and died there four years later. He was either murdered, or killed in trying to escape. Richard III suffered himself when his only son Edward, Prince of Wales, died mysteriously at the age of eight.

Old and well known as these stories are they serve as an astonishing contrast to the lives of Royal children of the present day. The safety and security of Prince Charles and Princess Anne are, today, taken for granted. Due to advances in education and science their lives are freer, more democratic and imbued with a new spirit of adventure.

Prince Charles and his little sister travel happily about the country in trains, by car and on foot. Their nursery and schoolroom are run on modern democratic lines. The new spirit of adventure exemplified when the children embarked on the Royal Yacht—sailing the high seas in order to meet their parents at Tobruk. No Royal child of such tender years has ever before left the shores of England to travel abroad. It was an important journey pointing a finger to the future. Freedom of travel and the telescoping of time in covering great distances will bring Prince Charles and Princess Anne, as they grow older, into personal touch with all kinds of people all over the world. They will give, and be given, new experiences, gain wider vision, and in consequence should have a deep sympathy and understanding of the joys and difficulties of life.

Returning from their first great Travel-adventure, on which they were accompanied by their head nurse, under nurse and governess, Prince Charles and Princess Anne settled down again to their normal

In Clarence House gardens

everyday life. Mrs Lightbody in charge of the nursery, Miss Peebles, as governess, looking after Prince Charles' school curriculum.

Mrs Lightbody, a Scotswoman, although unmarried, is given the prefix 'Mrs' in view of the importance of the position which she holds—all through her training of the children she has kept in the forefront of her mind the fact that the happiness and joy of living depends on learning how to make the best use of life.

It may be thought quite unreasonable to compare the life and training of Royal children with that of children born into ordinary work-a-day homes. The Royal child, on the surface, seems to have so much that is denied to the ordinary child, but really there is only one great fundamental difference and that difference is greatly to the disadvantage of the Royal baby. An ordinary child is free— free in the future to choose his own pursuits, enjoy to the full any gifts with which he may be endowed, and to marry where his heart wills. The Royal child, on the other hand, has to live his life in the public service. Should he be inspired to be a great musician, painter, architect or engineer, whatever his gifts, he cannot give up his life to his heart's desire. The country and his people must come first; his natural gifts or perhaps even genius, must be subservient and take second place. This naturally involves a discipline and self-sacrifice throughout the whole of his life which is quite unknown to the average, ordinary child. Then, too, in the distance looms the shadow of the Royal Marriage Act. The Royal child is dedicated from the moment of birth. He, too, has to face his share of the fierce light

At Birkhall, listening to the music of the pipes

Profound interest in the workings of a watch

of publicity that beats upon the Throne, so, every action, almost every word comes under the microscope of public scrutiny; indeed it is hardly an exaggeration that as the Royal child grows older, he is free only in thought. Here then is the basic difference. The Royal child has to live his life in the *public* interest; the life of any other child is governed by *personal* interest.

This difference does not call for any variation in the matters of feeding, clothing, health and so forth. In each case, sound and healthy upbringing naturally calls for intelligence and firmness. This means self-sacrifice and unselfishness on the part of those in charge of the child's welfare. It is here that the upbringing of these Royal children may serve as an example to parents.

In discipline and education there is a difference, but it is one of degree rather than of kind. As to discipline, one of the most important tenets the Royal child must learn is that he cannot have his own way or follow all his wishes, so that in the end, consideration for others and for the public service becomes not only a habit but a natural way of life. The main difference lies in the manner of education. Any ordinary person can follow, within limits, whatever calling he pleases. The education of the Royal child is bounded by his standing. It has to follow certain lines to fit him for his future position. Royalty is his 'vocation' and however strongly he may want to follow a natural bent he cannot indulge it to the full.

The Royal Marriage Act is still in force which means that freedom of choice even in marriage is not always permitted. It is one more of the sacrifices demanded of Royalty. Happily, today there is, in spite of this Act, greater freedom of choice. This was seen in the marriage of King George VI and the Queen Mother and in that of the Queen and the Duke of Edinburgh. When, therefore, Prince Charles came into the world at 9.14 in the evening of 14 November

Princess Anne enjoys playing with her doll and pram

Her Majesty and her children in the grounds of Balmoral

1948 he shared one advantage with less highly placed children; he was born into a home in which love reigned. Princess Elizabeth and the Duke of Edinburgh were still living at Buckingham Palace; they had not yet moved into Clarence House, their London home. Prince Charles was born at the Palace and spent the first few months of his life there. The great rejoicing throughout the Commonwealth showed the deep affection there was for the King and Queen and for Princess Elizabeth in the hearts of the people. The news of the birth of Prince Charles was greeted with great enthusiasm in the United States and in Eire, as well as in many foreign countries.

The old schoolroom at Buckingham Palace was turned into a nursery for the little Prince. Many of his baby clothes were made by his great-grandmother, the late Queen Mary, and Princess Elizabeth knitted most of his first woollies. On 15 December 1948 came the great event of the christening.

An interesting historical fact which sometimes escapes notice is that Prince Charles' ancestry goes back to King Henry VII not only through his mother but through his father, the Duke of Edinburgh, as well. A more remarkable fact still is that he goes back to the same king through all his *four grandparents*. The Duke of Edinburgh's father was Prince Andrew of Greece and his mother was Princess Alice. Prince Andrew was descended from George II, so too was Princess Alice (who was a great-granddaughter of Queen Victoria). Thus, through the Georges and James I of England, they both go

The Queen enjoying a joke with her small son

back to Henry VII. On the Queen's side, her father, King George VI, traces his descent back to Queen Victoria and so on back to Henry VII. Her mother, Queen Elizabeth the Queen Mother, who was a Bowes-Lyon, is a direct descendant of Mary, Queen of France, who was a daughter of Henry VII.

By Letters patent of 9 November 1948 Charles was given the title of Prince, and the style of Royal Highness. These were conferred upon him in view of his mother's position, as heir presumptive. Now, as heir apparent to the Throne, H.R.H. Prince Charles assumes the title of Duke of Cornwall, in accordance with the Charter of Edward III in 1337. The heir apparent is born Duke of Cornwall, but the titles of Prince of Wales and Earl of Chester are bestowed upon him later by the reigning sovereign. The first Prince of Wales and Earl of Chester was created by Edward I at a Parliament held in Lincoln on 7 February 1301. When the title, Prince of Wales, is conferred upon him by the Queen, Prince Charles will sign his name *Charles P.*

This little Prince with the weight of tradition on his shoulders, has to have the foundation of his character laid in his earliest years. This is a grave responsibility both for his mother and his nurses. Although many duties which most mothers do themselves have, in the case of a Royal child, to be carried out by his nurses, the main responsibility in the end is with the mother whose wishes have to be obeyed.

The Queen was fortunate that in her early years her mother, as Duchess of York, was able to devote a great deal of personal attention to the upbringing of her two children, Princess Elizabeth and Princess Margaret. Much of Her Majesty's character can be attributed to the loving care she received from her mother in those early years. The Queen has shown how she herself has profited by this loving care. It is mirrored in the charm and naturalness of her own children.

In two ways the Queen has been faced with a more difficult task than had her mother in the upbringing of her children. As Princess

Smile please !

Elizabeth, she was heir presumptive to the Throne and the public made much greater demands on her time than they did upon her mother at the same age. As reigning sovereign her responsibilities increased and are far greater than those of her mother when she was consort of the late George VI.

To make her task still more difficult, during the first two and three-quarter years of Prince Charles' life, the Duke of Edinburgh was in the Navy. Princess Anne was born and Princess Elizabeth, naturally wishing to spend some time with her husband stationed at Malta, found her time and energy divided between three duties—

Trial   Combined operations

Determination

Princess Anne's third birthday photograph

Prince Charles, nearing his fifth birthday

those to her country, her husband and her children. Due to these circumstances, although Her Majesty personally supervised her babies' routine, serious responsibilities fell to the head nurse and other members of the household.

Like so many other mothers, the Queen carries out the task of the upbringing of her children partly in person and partly by proxy, just as mothers who can afford it, have a nurse or some help in the home. The difference is simply one of degree. Today even the mothers who cannot afford indoor help and are over-burdened by household work and cares or have to go out to work to make ends meet, also bring up their children partly in person and partly by proxy. They can enjoy the services of a nurse at the day nurseries where they can leave their children in safe hands. The important point is not so much *who* performs the duties but the kind of up-bringing and how it is carried out.

It is not surprising that many nannies enjoy to the end of their lives the love of those babies they so carefully tended in their early years. A nurse's position is always one of responsibility, particularly

Trying to do the heavy work

is this so where their charge is a Royal child. To be chosen as Nannie to a prospective King of England is not an unmixed blessing. Like a general in command of an army, the honour is attended by ever-present responsibility.

Mrs Lightbody was appointed to take charge of Prince Charles when he was a month old. She had behind her twenty-four years' experience in nurseries before going to Princess Elizabeth as her head nurse. Previously she had already seen service with the Royal Family, as head nurse to the two sons of the Duke and Duchess of Gloucester.

When Mrs Lightbody had been head of the Royal Nurseries for nearly two years, Princess Anne was born on 15 August 1950 at Clarence House. She was christened by the Archbishop of Canterbury at Buckingham Palace and named Anne Elizabeth Alice Louise.

Mrs Lightbody looks very much younger than her many years of service would suggest. She makes a point of keeping up with the modern advances made in her profession. She also recognizes that the secret of the successful upbringing of happy and contented children is *routine*. Regular habits, such as bedtime, morning sleep, outings, and simple punctual meals must be rigidly observed. If a child is accustomed to go to bed at 6 o'clock, it is most upsetting for him to be kept up until 7.30 p.m. to be shown off to some friend or relative. The child does not benefit; it is really only a selfish whim of the parent and the temptation should be firmly resisted. The over-excitement may result in a bad night of crying and fretfulness. One effect upon the child of rigid routine is a feeling of security. It really *is* the hallmark of a good mother and of a good nurse to give the child this feeling of confidence. A baby will gain security and happiness not only by regular habits but in such things as the way it is held, being comfortable and dry and in so many small loving ways. With this confident happiness and contentment comes ready obedience—and this is the foundation stone of successful upbringing.

Prince Charles was seven-and-a-half months old when Princess

Persuading Sugar to look nice too

Elizabeth and the Duke of Edinburgh moved into Clarence House, their London home.

At Buckingham Palace their rooms are on the second floor. They consist of a nursery, a sitting-room for Nana (as Mrs Lightbody is affectionately called in the home circle), two bedrooms, a bathroom, airing cupboard, and a small kitchen. The decorations are simple but attractive, the main colouring being mushroom and eau-de-nil. Always two vases full of beautiful flowers lighten the austerity of the nursery. Among the toys to be seen are two model Cornish cottages with which, now she is old enough, Princess Anne loves to play. The furniture is simple but there are two delightful cabinets; one belongs to Prince Charles and the other to Princess Anne. Their great-grandmother, Queen Mary, gave one of these cabinets to each of her great-grandchildren in which to keep their special treasures. The one she gave to Princess Anne is made of Australian mahogany. The top is enclosed by glass doors and the base contains drawers and cupboard room. In the upper part Princess Anne keeps a miniature tea service and two lovely little gold elephants, their trappings enamelled in glowing colours; these were a gift to her from her godfather, Lord Mountbatten.

Besides the Cornish cottages which were a wedding present to the Queen, the children love to play with another of her presents which she had as a little girl. This is the famous cottage given to her on her sixth birthday by the people of Wales, called 'Y Brwthyn Bach to Gweltt', which means 'The little house with the thatched roof'. As a child of six can comfortably walk about inside it, naturally it is too big for any nursery and stands in the grounds of the Royal Lodge at Windsor. It is a complete house with electric light, running water

Young musicians

Rest after play

and a bathroom. The children love dusting, tidying up, making the beds and playing at tea-parties and also enjoy themselves turning the electric lights on and off.

Back in the nursery Prince Charles' teddy bear may still occasionally be seen in a chair by the window. Although Prince Charles now has more grown-up toys, Teddy still reigns supreme and is regularly taken to bed.

The keynote of the nurseries is simplicity. The late King George VI and Queen Elizabeth, the Queen's mother, showed their feelings towards everything that affected their people by sacrifices and self economies. Her Majesty has followed their example as closely as possible. Considering the huge returns provided today from the Crown Lands, this is even more commendable especially in view of

Happy in the garden

her youth, the fullness of the life she leads and her obvious joy in doing it.

From birth, Prince Charles' feeding has been much the same as that of any other child of a similar age. Mothers, no doubt, will have their own personal views on this important subject, but if a plain and wholesome diet is followed, then the child should be contented and sleep well, as is the case with Prince Charles and Princess Anne.

From about one month old a baby should be given food every four hours throughout the day. During the night, from 10 p.m. to 6 a.m., he should not be fed. Should he wake during the night, his mother or nurse should see that he is comfortable and dry. If not, she should make him so *without* lifting him from the cot. She might

perhaps give him a sip of water but unless he is ill or has wind, he must *never be picked up*. This rule should be rigidly adhered to. No one is quicker than a baby to realize that if he cries loud enough, someone will come and give him an extra feed, pick him up, or rock his cot or pram. An extra feed is definitely bad for the child (unless specially ordered by the doctor) and rocking creates a vicious circle; the baby, when put back in his cot, will start to cry again in an attempt to get the performance repeated—and the next night he will remember and start all over again. Screaming is the means a spoilt child uses for drawing attention to himself. In extra feeds, picking up and rocking, a child is definitely being spoilt. A baby is an intelligent being and soon develops the 'crying-waking' habit by all this fuss just to get his own way. Under conditions of crowded living, it is difficult to be firm on this point but unless one tackles it, the baby will become a tyrant. He becomes a burden to his parents instead of being a pleasure. If a firm line is really taken, the habit of waking through the night can be conquered in a week or, at most, a month.

Whilst on the subject of crying, every healthy baby cries a little during the day. This is definitely good 'exercise'; it develops the lungs and creates all sorts of extra muscular movements. Provided the baby is well, comfortable and dry, let him have a good cry. A mother or a nurse can soon distinguish between the three different types of crying; these are the cries of hunger, pain or temper.

Returning to the subject of feeding. Cow's milk is generally accepted as the best substitute for mother's milk but as it varies from place to place, it is not altogether satisfactory to use it for the bottles of a child who does much travelling. In such cases it is much better to use powdered milk which can be relied upon as safe and has the advantage of being constant in its content. To help in bone building, it is a good thing to add halibut oil to the diet from the time the child is one month old. Starting with one drop, this can be increased gradually to six drops a day. At six months old, the mid-day bottle should be given up and in its place bone and vegetable

Queen Elizabeth the Queen Mother giving sweets to her grandchildren at the Royal Lodge, Windsor

Sunshine

broth substituted. This should be given with a cup and spoon so that the baby becomes accustomed from an early age to this method of feeding. At about the same age, the 10 p.m. bottle should also be given up. With regard to both of these changes, no hard and fast rule can be set as they depend upon the progress of the individual child.

After the age of six months, orange juice is a healthy addition to the diet but this should *not* be given first thing in the morning. If taken on an empty tummy, it may upset the child's liver; a drink of water is much better if an early drink is needed. Bottles should be given up as soon as possible, probably by about the ninth month, and the baby put on to a more solid diet. Here again, one cannot be too dogmatic as the change will depend on how early the baby has taken to a cup and spoon. The ninth month is generally a critical period, not only from the point of view of feeding but in teething as well. The right road of plain wholesome food makes for good health and easy teething. The road of wrong and indiscriminate feeding brings tummy-ache, crying, bad-temper, difficult teething and even convulsions in its wake. Too great a stress cannot be laid on the correct way of feeding a child at any age. If a young mother is uncertain about her baby's diet, any infant clinic will gladly give her help and sound advice.

A baby's diet should now include some type of green vegetable and fruit every day and, of course, a good deal of milk. As he grows older, the diet can be varied but it must be kept plain. As far as fats and sugar are concerned, every child is individual. Fat agrees with

The Queen Mother as a guest of the children at the little Welsh Cottage

Sitting on the terrace of the Royal Lodge

some but occasionally completely upsets other babies. Sugar, too, cannot always be taken satisfactorily.

Prince Charles has been brought up on the sort of plain and wholesome diet suggested above; as a result, he is a good sleeper and a contented child. Being a healthy child, he can eat almost anything but he is not allowed rich cakes or pastries. His sweets are strictly rationed and he is only given one or two a day, usually at mid-day, never at night. Princess Anne had a special diet during part of her babyhood to which Nana rigidly adhered. The result of this care is shown in the strong and bonnie little girl she is today.

The Commonwealth of New Zealand issue health stamps which sell at 3d and 2d each. One-third of the proceeds go to a fund for providing health camps in the country for ailing, weak and under-nourished children. Since these stamps were first issued in 1931, the

Interest in a toy

design has always symbolized healthy childhood. The issue brought out in October 1950 contained the portraits of Princess Elizabeth and Prince Charles. This was no formal compliment but a tribute to the fact that Prince Charles is the picture of health.

Because all the world loves a baby, Royal babies become objects of very special interest—this naturally adds to the trials of their nannies. Women and children, and even men, hang about in the hope of catching a glimpse of Prince Charles or Princess Anne. Nana has continually to think of ways and means of avoiding too much publicity for her Royal charges. This is not because the Queen minds her children being seen but as Prince Charles has not been told who he is—or rather of his importance in the scheme of things— it would be bad for him or for Princess Anne to think that they were constantly the centre of attention. Nana has, therefore, to devise

plans to give the children their outings away from the public.
Whilst at Clarence House, Princess Anne used to sleep in the
garden while Prince Charles had his usual morning outing, generally

At their own front door

in the Park. Here he sometimes fed the ducks or watched the Chang-
ing of the Guard. On his return, he was given a drink of fruit juice,
after which he had his mid-day rest until 1 o'clock. In the afternoon,

ong the daffodils

Greeting Rear-Admiral A. G. V. Hubback before embarking

both children went out either in their prams or farther afield in a car.

So democratic are the nurseries that the children are never told of their exalted rank; the prefixes Prince or Princess are not used in the nurseries. The children are simply Charles and Anne. In spite of the glamour that otherwise surrounds their lives, the children accept their simple way of living. Some people are sceptical about this but children invariably take their 'way of life' for granted. There is nothing to let them know that the crowds do not wave to the little sons and daughters of some other people when they go out, or that station-masters do not stand cap in hand for other children as well. It is the only life they know; therefore it is, at present, to them lived by other children. Prince Charles is now getting to the end of his nursery days. His training for the life of service he will be called upon to live, has already started and his little feet will

With the Queen Mother and Princess Margaret on their way to the yacht

carefully and gently be led along the straight and difficult road which he is to follow.

In spite of the changes which have taken place in recent years in the political structure of the British Commonwealth, two of the greatest demands upon Royalty remain as exacting as ever. One of these is the call of travel, not only all over Great Britain but throughout the Colonies and Dominions. The other is the need to be pleasant

On board at last : Miss Peebles and Mrs Lightbody in attendance

and smiling under all and any circumstances. To be taught how to meet these necessary and difficult demands is part of the early training of a prince or princess. It looks as if Prince Charles and Princess Anne seem to have acquired very young the natural ease of manner which bridges so many troubles.

Prince Charles is devoted to his little sister. Like so many brothers and sisters, the Prince and Princess are unalike in character. Prince

Earl and Lady Mountbatten arriving with the children at Mal

Paddling in the rock pool

Charles is a rather thoughtful and serious child, with a good sense of humour, and is very malleable and easily trained. Princess Anne, young as she is, is more like quick-silver, restless and very intelligent for her age. Both children were forward babies, though Princess Anne as a small baby was more delicate than Prince Charles. They both cut their first teeth at about the same age, between eight and nine months. This is not a sign of backwardness, as some mothers think, but means that the mother has been really cared for and has taken care of herself before the babies were born. The baby's general bone formation is extra strong in consequence and the teeth, being sturdier, take longer to come through. Prince Charles is now getting beyond the stage of nursery rhymes but he still loves picture books and is beginning to read his own story books. He can now sign his name really well, an accomplishment of which he is very proud.

In the early morning before getting up both children have picture books to look at and each in their separate rooms have a lovely time singing songs and nursery rhymes to themselves. The only time that Princess Anne is really as still as a mouse is when someone reads her a story or sings her a song. Both children show signs of being musical. Prince Charles' speciality is listening to organ music. He will sit quite still in rapturous enjoyment. He also makes music for himself on his toy trumpet. Prince Charles is now very much the big brother doing lessons with his governess, Miss Katherine Peebles, a Scotswoman who has been entrusted with

Discovering more pools

Happily together, at last, on the Royal Yacht

this part of his upbringing, and has had special training to fit her for her important post.

To the Queen and the Duke of Edinburgh, family life in the Royal home is all important. The children live simply and are treated and encouraged to behave like ordinary little boys and girls.

Between 9 and 9.15 in the morning, Prince Charles and Princess Anne go down to see their mother and father and stay with them until it is time for their rest or morning outing. Every evening without fail, unless public duties intervene, the Queen and the Duke go to the nursery to help bath the children and put them to bed.

Being safely escorted ashore by Sir Gerald Creasy, Governor of Malta, and Lt-General Sir Frederick Browning

A great favourite of Prince Charles is his grandmother, the Queen Mother. His little face lights up when he sets eyes on her and he runs to meet her. The Queen, like her parents, is sincerely religious. Truth and faith shine out in her kindliness to others, in the simplicity of her home life and in the upbringing of her children.

On the death of his dearly loved grandfather, George VI, and the accession of his mother, Princess Elizabeth, to the throne of England, Prince Charles became the heir apparent and automatically became the Duke of Cornwall.

Prince Charles was three years old and his sister, Princess Anne, a mere baby when their young mother, at the age of twenty-five, became Queen Elizabeth II. They were too small to grasp the differences this would make to their lives, as well as to those of their parents. One of the understandable and happy-making changes was that their father, the Duke of Edinburgh, no longer went to sea; their mother no longer went away to Malta, and home life was a complete and secure family affair.

Another very important and exciting change was moving from Clarence House into Buckingham Palace. The new nurseries had to be explored—the floor on which they lie was fresh territory. Part of the Palace and the gardens the children knew well, having so often visited their grandparents, Queen Elizabeth the Queen Mother, and the late King George VI. The nurseries have been newly decorated in pink and white.

Although the demands upon the Queen's time are much greater than at Clarence House, she still goes up to the nurseries whenever she has a free moment and makes a special point of being there at bath time. The children still go down to the dining-room every morning after breakfast to see their parents. In the nursery corridor there is a red carpet and this is often turned into a playground— for playing ball, and games.

Prince Charles, though full of spirit, is a seriously minded child, malleable and good tempered but with a great sense of fun, clearly enjoying simple practical jokes, not always thoroughly appreciated

Feeding nuts to an ape at Gibralta

Home at last

by Princess Anne. She is much more temperamental—never still, often up to mischief, very intelligent, quickly moved to laughter or tears, consequently not so easily led as Prince Charles.

At first, when Princess Anne was a baby, Prince Charles looked upon her as his own special possession. As she grew a little older, he took intense interest in the growing-up process. Such things as new teeth or new words added to her small vocabulary, absorbed him. As soon as she was able to stand and run, he treated her rather as another boy and she, of course, always wanted to do what 'Charles did' so they have grown into good playmates. Prince Charles has his own boy friends among whom Bruce Gillingham, son of the Chaplain of Windsor, is his special favourite. One day after he had been naughty and made Princess Anne cry, Nana made him stay in the nursery and Princess Anne was sent to play with Bruce in his stead—it is a lesson Prince Charles will not forget.

On his fifth birthday, Prince Charles put away many babyish things; the time had come to begin his training for kingship. Every morning Prince Charles has his lessons in the schoolroom whilst Princess Anne goes for a walk and has her morning rest. Lessons last about an hour and a half and, at present, are not too strenuous; in fact much the same as those of any other little boy of his age.

As soon as a small boy begins to leave his nursery days behind him, he instinctively turns to his father for guidance. During his babyhood, his mother is his all in all, to comfort pain and bring solace over a broken toy; in fact, all his small troubles are taken to Mummie. During babyhood as a rule the father is a dear, but less approachable, figure in the background. Reaching the age of five or six, a boy begins (if properly trained) to stand on his own feet. He has been taught not to cry when hurt and to be a man. Automatically begins the hero-worship of his father, who is big and strong in the eyes of his little son. The boy learns to wield a bat, throw a ball properly, and how to kick and dribble a football—that is if he is lucky enough to have a father who is a companion and a mother who will step aside a little and lose part of her possessiveness. It is during the next few years that a father's responsibility is paramount. After that, a boy relies on school friendships and the teaching of his masters. Home influence has done its work and holidays generally become the highlights of a child's life because during them, a great many of the old home restrictions are relaxed.

The Royal children have to learn control and manners far beyond their years which ages them in some ways and certainly puts them in a class apart. The pictures taken after they had met their parents at Tobruk and when they were all together at Malta, show Prince Charles as the perfectly mannered child. The chivalrous

Pets Corner at the Zoo

control he shows in helping his little sister down the steps, all points to the care and repeated teaching of Mrs Lightbody and Miss Peebles. The wonderful thing is that it becomes a natural trait—consideration for others. Good manners are, of course, founded on unselfish thought for other people. Her Majesty, when at Tobruk, not having seen her children for over five months, did not hasten, hurry or avoid a single one of the duties which she had undertaken to fulfil, nor did she in any manner indicate that the one place in the world she wanted to be was on board the Royal Yacht. What a rewarding moment it must have been when she and the Duke stepped on to the deck of the *Britannia* to be welcomed by a rush of small feet and soft arms round their necks. Her Majesty and the Duke have had to miss much of the entrancing time in the babyhood of their children. When Prince Charles was a baby, his father was stationed hundreds of miles away in Malta and his mother was called upon to divide

En route for Balmoral

Full of fun, waving to the crowds

her time into three parts—between him, his father and her own public duties. After Princess Anne was born, in August 1950, Princess Elizabeth (as Her Majesty then was) had to leave both babies behind, just like other young Service wives. But due to the burden of her numerous public duties in addition to all else, an outcry went up from her people that the strain put upon her was too great. Nevertheless, in October 1951, she and the Duke agreed to a Canadian Tour and the parents again had to leave their babies.

Shortly before they were due to sail to Canada, the Queen's father, King George VI, became very ill and had to undergo a serious operation. In consequence, the journey by sea had to be cancelled.

This sea voyage would have been a restful holiday for Princess Elizabeth. Although the Canadian people generously offered to postpone the Tour, it was decided that as soon as her father was out of immediate danger, the Royal couple should make up the time by flying the Atlantic. They were away just over a month and during that time travelled right across the Dominion and back sandwiching in a forty-five-hour visit to Washington. They travelled after leaving the shores of England by air, sea, train and car, 16,462 miles—over 4,000 miles a week, an average of well over 700 miles a day. The strain of this tour alone must have been gruelling but to all Princess Elizabeth had to do was added the constant and intense worry about her father. By the time the Royal couple arrived in Washington, it was being remarked in the Press how tired and exhausted she looked—but still she smiled and made charming speeches; particularly was this so of the one made to the Canadian people on the eve of departure. The Princess spoke in both French and English; this speech was relayed to us in England and was a delight to hear.

Whilst the Duke and the Princess were still in Canada, the medical advisers to George VI decided that although he had made a wonderful recovery, he was not yet strong enough to undertake the rigours of the tour to Australia and New Zealand which had been previously decided upon. King George asked Princess Elizabeth and the Duke of Edinburgh to go in his stead. To this they at once agreed. Such a short time at home with her babies, only about seven weeks, before the Royal couple were off again to the other side of the world. This journey had a tragic ending. On a cold January morning, King George VI was at the airfield to wave to them and say good-bye. It was his last good-bye to her—the tragic news of his death was broken to the Princess by her husband at Sagano Lodge, a house given to her as a wedding gift by the people of Kenya. Hurried preparations were set afoot to fly Princess Elizabeth, now Queen Elizabeth, back from East Africa to England. Her Majesty arrived home on 7 February 1952; a sad young figure dressed in black, she walked with slow dignity down the gangway

from the aeroplane on to the airfield to be received by Mr Winston Churchill, Mr Attlee, Mr Eden, and Lord Woolton. On the following day, the Queen attended her Accession Council at St James's Palace.

Due to the death of his grandfather, King George VI, little Prince Charles had become the heir apparent, next in succession to the

Throne of England. This sad and tragic time passed gently over the children's heads as they played happily in their nursery.

Another event of great sadness and personal, as well as national loss, was the death at the great age of eighty-five on 24 March 1953 of Queen Mary, Prince Charles' and Princess Anne's great-grandmother. Queen Mary had been a loved figure in our midst for so long, it was almost impossible to believe that she had passed away. Often she used to go to tea in the nursery at Clarence House and the children used to visit her at home in Marlborough House. Much sadness had touched her life, and her grandchildren and great-grandchildren were a continual source of joy and happiness to her. Queen Mary was buried in St George's Chapel.

During this time of sad loss for Her Majesty, preparations had

ving good-bye to an unseen friend at Ballater Station

been going forward for her Coronation which was to take place on 2 June 1953, a year and a quarter after the Queen's accession to the Throne. This may seem a lengthy lapse of time but the machinery needed to bring this event to a successful conclusion is gigantic. In London alone fifteen separate Committees were set up to deal with the various details such as preparing the Abbey, building the great Annexe, decorations in the Abbey and throughout the streets of London, the erection of stands, the ordering of materials, the camping and housing of extra troops and police specially drafted into London for the occasion. The details were legion and the preparations carefully studied and successfully carried out. At the head of all these Committees was the premier duke and earl of England, Earl Marshal, the Duke of Norfolk. At the Coronation rehearsals, his wife, the Duchess, stood proxy for Her Majesty. The Duke was determined that the mishaps that took place at Queen Victoria's Coronation should in no way be repeated. For all the difficult and worrying details, this one man was responsible. He succeeded beyond all expectation. The Coronation was unique in that it was the first ever to be televised. We, in our homes, were able to view this awe-inspiring spectacle, not only the long drives through the streets of London but to be present at the actual service in the Abbey. The Service of Holy Communion and the Anointing being considered too sacred, were withheld from the viewers in their homes. No one who saw the ceremony on television could ever forget Her Majesty— a tiny figure against the vastness of the Abbey, serious, dignified, inspired, filling the air—even in our own rooms—with an atmosphere of sacred devoutness. Everyone must have prayed, as she had requested, that she might be given wisdom and strength to carry out her solemn promises. The determination of Her Majesty herself to fulfil her vows could almost tangibly be felt. There seemed to be a force inspiring her. Television sets, the material side of life, disappeared from the room—it was flooded with an uplifting religious fervour that was unforgettable.

Prince Charles and Princess Anne were considered too young to stand the strain of the long hours in the Abbey but Prince Charles was especially brought to Westminster to see his mother actually crowned. He sat between his grandmother, Queen Elizabeth the

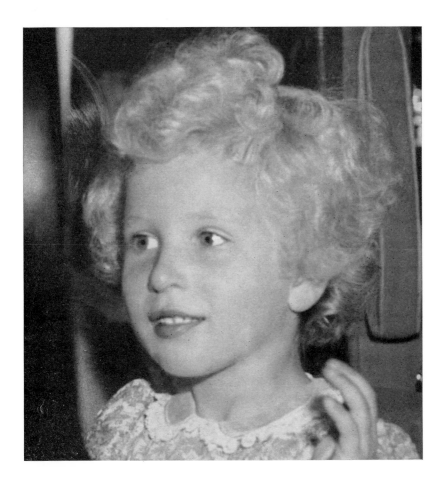

Queen Mother, and his aunt, Princess Margaret. He was intensely interested and asked many questions during the short time he was allowed to be present. It must have been an exciting day for both children—seeing their mother setting forth in the coach to go to the

Four years old

Six years old

Abbey and returning in the glass coach with her crown upon her head, just like a lovely fairy queen; the crowds and crowds of people all waiting in front of Buckingham Palace; the colourful decorations; the soldiers in uniform; so much to watch and see from the windows of Buckingham Palace. Then finally going out on to the balcony hearing the cheers of the people, and their mother the centre of all the excitement. An unforgettable day for Her Majesty's two small children, ending with the magnificent fly past by the R.A.F.

Prince Charles and Princess Anne for the next few months lived quietly at Buckingham Palace and Windsor Castle, with the usual summer holiday at Balmoral. Here they love to be. They go for walks into the village and are allowed to buy sweets at the village shop. They talk to the villagers and make new friends and greet old ones. The restrictions that have to be imposed in London are relaxed and the children revel in their freedom. Actions which to ordinary children are everyday occurrences, are exciting to the little brother and sister.

Then a cloud darkened their young horizons—their parents were again to leave them, this time to go away and be away longer than ever before. The latter fact they did not realize. Naturally time is a difficult factor for a small child to grasp but the parting—that they understood. So soon, only five months after the Coronation, on 23 November 1953, the Queen and the Duke of Edinburgh set forth on their now famous World Tour. They were to be away nearly six months. Six months is almost a lifetime in a growing baby—the incredible changes watched so fondly by every parent, the young Royal couple were to miss. Princess Anne during this time grew from a baby into an entrancing little girl. These two fascinating children, fascinating into whatever walk of life they had been born, have completely captured the public's affection. Their naturalness and good manners have endeared them to everyone. It must have been a heart-rending wrench to their parents to have to leave them behind, especially as they had to travel so far away, right round the world, before they saw them again.

Waiting at Waterloo Station to welcome home Queen Elizabeth the Queen Mother from her visit to Canada and the United States

It is a curious fact that a section of the public seem to think of Royalty as people 'apart'. They do not imbue them with loving hearts moved by joy or anguish, as are ordinary human beings. This probably is due to the intense training in public self-control that they have to undergo. Their feelings of joy, anger or anguish are only suppressed from the all-seeing public eye. Their emotions are all there, just as are ours.

Many years ago, Queen Mary had to leave her children when they were very young. An eye-witness told me that whilst keeping her features controlled and serene, tears rained down her cheeks unheralded and uncheckable.

The children, in the meantime, whilst naturally missing their parents intensely, were left in good and loving hands. Their so dearly loved grandmother, Elizabeth the Queen Mother, spent all the time she could spare only too willingly with them. Their aunt, Princess Margaret, too, spent many hours of her free time with them. Mrs Lightbody, the under nurses, and Miss Peebles all contributed in doing their best to fill the abysmal gap left by the nation-necessary departure of the Queen and the Duke of Edinburgh.

Their parents had been away so long that the children must have begun to wonder whenever they were to see them again. One day the marvellous news was told them that they were to set sail on the high seas in the Royal Yacht *Britannia* to meet the Queen and the Duke of Edinburgh at Tobruk in North Africa, and that the united family were to travel back to England together. On 14 April 1954 the most exciting event of their young lives arrived and they embarked from Portsmouth in the *Britannia*. With them went Mrs Lightbody, Miss Peebles and their under nurse Mabel Anderson.

Luckily the weather was perfect. The children followed their usual routine except that, on board the yacht, Prince Charles and Princess Anne found a completely new type of freedom—the ship was their world.

Four sailors, Able Seaman R. Chorlton, Leading Seaman L. E. Booker, Leading Stoker Mechanic Charles Rutter, and Leading

Off for the Christmas Holidays

Stoker Richard McKeown, were detailed for this new, delightful and unexpected duty to keep the children out of harm's way. This duty they nobly performed but soon these entrancing babies persuaded the stokers into playing games of all sorts, one of the greatest attractions being hide and seek. Princess Anne had her dolls but these only received casual attention; she far preferred running about the deck barefoot helping to swab it down with her own deck tools. Alongside her working away hard was her brother, Prince Charles. By the time they arrived at Tobruk, they must have looked the picture of nut brown health.

Meanwhile, the Queen and the Duke of Edinburgh, fulfilling the last duties of their tour, finally too arrived at Tobruk. On the balcony when being entertained by King Idris of Libya, the Queen and the

Duke got their first glimpse of the *Britannia* riding at anchor in the Bay. For five long crowded months, Her Majesty and the Duke had waited for this day, but on land there were still some public duties to perform before they could board the Royal Yacht. The moment came at last. Her Majesty and Prince Philip stepped on board quickly mounting the stairway which led up to the Stateroom where Prince Charles and Princess Anne were waiting for them in a tiptoe of excitement. The children and their parents later came out on deck, all looking radiantly happy, excited and—at last, united.

There were now only two more places to be visited, Malta and Gibraltar, before the Queen was home with us again. At both these places the children were allowed to land, much to the joy of the crowds assembled to greet the Royal family.

Gibraltar and its legendary Barbary apes gave the children one of the biggest thrills of their lives. They were allowed not only to go and see the apes but to feed them. Prince Charles, from his nearly two years' seniority, approached them at first with reasoned care, but Princess Anne skipped about among them with no apprehension whatsoever. She doubled up with shouts of laughter when one of the apes jumped on to the shoulder of an official in charge. One actually used Princess Anne's shoulder as a spring-board to get from one perch to another. The little Princess whizzed round quickly to see what had touched her; seeing nothing, she looked a little bewildered, then discovering the ape above her, smiled happily and fed it with nuts. There is, of course, a legend attaching to these apes. It is that so long as there is one left on the Rock, Gibraltar will remain in our possession. They have rather naturally been well looked after and have become quite tame and friendly.

In spite of threatened 'incidents' reported in the Spanish Press should Her Majesty land at Gibraltar, nothing untoward occurred but anxiety for her safety was felt throughout the world. It was with great relief and joy that the news of her safe departure on her final journey home was received.

On Saturday, 15 May 1954, the s.e. corner of the coast of England

At a meet of the West Norfolk hounds ; Prince Charles proudly astride

was alert at dawn. People armed with binoculars crowded down to the cliffs and beaches and little boats of all sorts put out to sea, not in the hope of even glimpsing the Queen and her family but to get perhaps a slightly misty view of the *Britannia,* moving gently at her anchorage about two miles out at sea off Margate. So the people of England started that day at dawn to pay their tribute of affection and to express their joyous happiness at the safe return of the Queen and her family to their own home land.

The yacht weighed anchor and steamed slowly up the Thames Estuary eventually arriving at Tower Bridge—the gateway to London proper. The story of this historic day is best told in pictures —the excitement, the crowds, the uniting of the whole Royal family, the Royal Barge moving slowly along the grey breast of the Thames, the Queen, the Duke and their children as well as Elizabeth, the Queen Mother, and Princess Margaret, all on board; the banks on either side lined with people cheering their hearts out in an effort to let the Queen know their unbounded delight in having her home once more; the drive through streets crowded to their utmost capacity from Westminster to Buckingham Palace; the almost uncontrollable crowds outside the Palace, calling for Her Majesty; the thunderous cheers of tumultuous joy on the Queen's appearance on the balcony with her husband and children—might well have been heard miles away. It must have been a rewarding day to the young Queen and her husband who had travelled so far and so triumphantly, working often day and night to bring a realization of the meaning to the words 'England and the Commonwealth'.

To the children it too must have been an exciting day. Both Prince Charles and Princess Anne took a lively interest in all that was going on, waving happily to the crowds and probably agreeing with them that, in spite of all the thrills of their sea voyage, it was lovely to be safe home again. God bless our beloved young Queen. God save our gracious Majesty, and all those whom she holds dear.

Princess Anne's eager excitement on sightin
Princess Margaret's plane returning from the West Indi